Minecraft with Steve

Steve Math

Copyright © 2015 by Steve Math. All rights reserved.

No part of this book may be duplicated, redistributed, or given away without prior consent from the author.

Disclaimer: This book is a work of fanfiction; it is not an official Minecraft book. It is not endorsed, authorized, licensed, sponsored, or supported by Mojang AB, Microsoft Corp. or any other entity owning or controlling rights to the Minecraft name, trademarks or copyrights.
Minecraft ®/TM & © 2009-2015 Mojang / Notch / Microsoft

All names, places, characters and all other aspects of the game mentioned from here on are trademarked and owned by their respective owners. Any other trademarks or company names mentioned in this book are the property of their respective owners and are only mentioned for identification purposes.

Special thanks to MadPixel for the font and Rymdnisse for the rigs.

Steve awoke in a brand new seed today. He is excited to be in this new world, so he wanders around for a bit. After exploring for an hour, he sees something in the distance. It looks like a village. "Hey, I should go check that out."

1. Steve arrives in the new village. The first building he stops by is the blacksmith because he knows there is a chest inside. "I should go get some free stuff!" He goes in to check out the chest and finds 10 apples, 20 carrots, 4 iron ingots, and 12 gold ingots. "Score!"

    a. If Steve decides to take only 5 apples and save the rest for later, how many apples would be remaining in the chest?

    b. Steve feels rather hungry. He decides to eat 4 carrots right away from the chest, how many carrots are left?

    c. The glittering gold caught Steve's eyes. He decides to take a total of 9 gold ingots from the chest, how many remains?

2. After visiting the blacksmith, Steve wanders over to a farm. He sees that the potatoes are ready for harvest, so he decides to help himself. There were a total of 20 potatoes.

   a. Steve harvests and takes away 5 potatoes, how many remains?

   b. He decides to harvest some more to save for later, just in case he gets hungry again. He takes another 3 potatoes, how many is left?

   c. The villager farmer came out and told Steve to take half of the remaining potatoes. What is half of the remaining or unharvested potatoes?

3. After gathering enough food, Steve goes to a villager to see what they have to trade. The villager had a wooden axe to trade, but he wanted Steve to give him 10 potatoes for it.

   a. If Steve had a total of 20 potatoes, how many will Steve have left after the trade?

   b. The villager also had a nice wooden sword for trade, but he wanted 1 gold ingot for it. Steve currently had 9 gold ingots. How many will remain after the trade?

   c. The last thing the villager had to trade was a pickaxe. For this item, he wanted 8 apples. Steve only had 5 apples at the time. How many more apples does Steve need for the trade?

4. Now that Steve has a sword to defend himself and an axe to chop wood, Steve decides to venture into the forest. He wants to build a shelter soon, so he walks up to some trees. Steve forgot to equip his axe, so he bashes the tree block until it broke.

   a. Assuming that each wood block takes 3 seconds to mine or break while unarmed, how long would it take Steve to mine/break 10 blocks of wood?

   b. Steve needs a lot of wood. How many seconds would it take to break/collect 50 blocks of wood?

   c. Suppose that Steve spent 120 seconds breaking wood blocks nonstop, how many blocks of wood would he have gone through?

5. Now that Steve has plenty of wood, he wants to build a house. It will be a basic square shaped house.

    a. If the base of the house is 10 by 10, how many blocks of wood would Steve need for just the base?

    b. What about the ceiling? How many blocks for the ceiling?

    c. If a wall is 4 blocks high and 8 blocks long, how many blocks would a wall need?

6. The house is starting to come along. Steve wants to let a little light in.

    a. If Steve wants each wall to have one window, how many windows should he put in?

    b. What if he wants to put in two windows per wall, how many windows would that be total?

    c. He changed his mind. He doesn't want the wall with the front door to have windows. So for the remaining walls, he wants two windows per wall. How many windows total?

7. Now that Steve has finished making the holes for the windows, he needs to actually make the glass pane for the windows. He sets out to build a furnace, but for that he needs stone. He finds some stone by digging nearby, but since he doesn't own a pickaxe, he has to break the stone by hand.

   a. Assuming it takes 8 seconds (rounded up) to break a stone block by hand, how long would it take Steve to break and collect 10 blocks of stone?

   b. If he only had 40 seconds, how many stone blocks could he break?

   c. If he had a wooden pickaxe and it took only 1 second to mine a stone block, how many blocks could Steve mine in 1 minute?

8. After collecting enough stone blocks, Steve returns to his newly built home. He forgot that he needed to add a door. To create a door, Steve would first need to build a crafting table. He uses the crafting kit in his inventory. 1 wood block can make 4 wood planks.

    a. Assuming Steve wants to make 20 wood planks, how many blocks of wood would he need?

    b. What if he wanted to make 28 wood planks, how many blocks for that many?

    c. Steve created 40 wood planks, how many blocks of wood did he use?

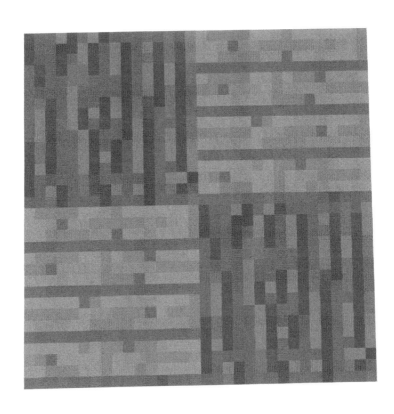

9. Now is time to build a crafting table. This item requires 4 wood planks to make.

   a. Assuming Steve wants to make 4 crafting tables, how many wood planks would he need?

   b. Steve actually wants to make 7 crafting tables so that he would have enough for future uses. How many wood planks would he need?

   c. Steve had a total of 40 wood planks, what is the maximum amount of crafting tables he can make?

10. It is time to craft the door. Steve needs more wood planks.

    a. Steve makes 4 more, then another 4 more, then another 4 more. How many wood planks did he just make total?

    b. What if Steve has 10 wood planks, but he misplaced 4 of them. How many would he have?

    c. What if he has 10 wood planks, then made 14 more. How many wood planks would he have total?

11. To make the door, Steve needs 6 wood planks for 3 doors.

    a. If Steve has a total of 18 wood planks, how many doors can he make?

    b. Steve is a bit extreme and wants a total of 30 doors, how many wood planks would he need?

    c. Steve ends up only building 6 doors, how many wood planks did he use?

12. Now with the door in place, the house is starting to look more like a house. It is time to build the furnace. For this item, Steve needs 8 stone blocks.

    a. He uses 8 blocks, then 8 more, then 8 more after that. How many furnaces did he make?

    b. He decides he wants to use 8 more blocks, then 8 more blocks after that. How many more furnaces did he make?

    c. So in total, Steve used 8 + 8 + 8 + 8 + 8 stone blocks. How many stone blocks is that total?

13. Steve placed down his new furnace and goes to look for some sand. He finds some nearby and breaks them with his hand.

    a. Steve wants to collect 20 + 20 blocks of sand. How much is that total?

    b. Sand takes 1 second to break, Steve wants to break 63 blocks. How many seconds will that take?

    c. Steve ends up with 42 blocks of sand in his inventory. He decides that is too much so drops out 12 blocks. How many blocks remain?

14. Ah, finally. Steve has everything he needs to start making glass. Steve puts 30 sand blocks into his furnace. He will be using wood planks as fuel, which can make 2 glasses per 1 plank. Using the furnace, 1 sand block input = 1 glass output.

    a. Steve initially puts in only 5 wood planks, how many glasses was he able to make?

    b. How many sand blocks remain?

    c. If he wants to finish the remaining sand blocks, how many wood planks would he need?

15. To make glass panes, Steve would use 6 glasses to make 16 glass panes.

    a. If he used 6 + 6 glasses, how many glass panes would he have made?

    b. If Steve had 16 glass panes, but drop and broke 5. How many would be left?

    c. From the question above, instead of dropping and breaking 5 glass panes, he broke 10, how many is left?

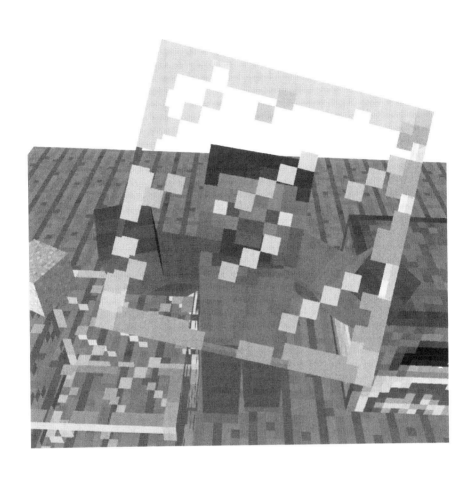

16. Steve puts all the glass panes in place. From the outside, his home looks basically done. It has been a pretty busy day for Steve, so he decides to go to bed early. "Whew! That was a lot of work for just some windows…"

    a. If Steve sleeps at 7 pm and wakes up at 5 am, how many hours did he sleep?

    b. Steve was really tired, so he actually slept from 7 pm to 9 am, how many hours is that total?

    c. What if he slept at 10 pm and woke up at 7 am? How many hours is that?

17. Steve wakes up bright and early because he couldn't sleep too well. Do you know why? Because he was missing a bed and had to sleep on the floor. "Ah! My back!" So, he starts off the day by building a bed. A bed requires wood planks and wools. Steve goes outside to look for sheep. He finds a flock of sheep and draws out his wooden sword.

   a. There are 10 sheep, but each sheep only has a 50% chance of dropping wool when it dies. How many wools will Steve collect from the sheep?

   b. His wooden sword does 5 Hearts of damage. If a sheep has 8 hearts, how many hits will it take to slay the sheep?

   c. There are 10 sheep, how many times does Steve have to swing his sword to slay the whole flock?

18. With lots of wool now, Steve returns home to build his bed. A bed requires 3 wood planks and 3 wools.

    a. If Steve has 12 wood planks and 12 wools, how many beds can he build?

    b. What if Steve has 3 wood planks and 15 wools, how many beds can he build?

    c. If Steve built 5 beds, how many wood planks and wools did he use total?

19. The bed is now in place; it is quite nice and comfortable. When Steve slayed the sheep, he picked up a lot of raw mutton. Each sheep dropped a raw mutton.

    a. If he killed 20 sheep, how many raw muttons did he pick up?

    b. If he killed only 50% of the 20 sheep, how many raw muttons is that total?

    c. Raw mutton tastes better cooked. 1 wooden plank will cook 2 raw muttons. If he has 14 raw muttons, how many wood planks will he need to cook them all?

20. Steve enjoyed the delicious cooked muttons. The furnace is nice and warm, but it still feels a bit cold, so Steve decides to craft some armor for himself. He sets out to look for horses or cows. He couldn't find any, instead he finds a bunch of rabbits. Each rabbit has a 25% chance of dropping a rabbit hide. He attacks the rabbits with his wooden sword. Each rabbit has 10 hearts and the sword does 5 hearts of damage.

   a. How many hits will a rabbit take before it dies?

   b. If Steve kills 12 rabbits, how many rabbit hides would he collect?

   c. Steve collected a total of 18 rabbit hides, how many rabbits did he kill?

21. Steve takes the rabbit hides and turn them into leather. Leather requires 4 rabbit hides to craft.

    a. What is the maximum amount of leathers Steve can craft if he has 20 rabbit hides?

    b. If Steve crafted a total of 7 leathers, he must have used how many rabbit hides?

    c. Steve used 8 rabbit hides, then another 8. What is the total amount of leather that he crafted?

22. Steve kept hunting and eventually ended up with 20 leathers. It is time to make some armor. A leather helmet requires 5 pieces of leather, a leather tunic requires 8 pieces of leather, a leather pant requires 7 pieces, and boots require 4 pieces.

   a. With Steve's inventory, which one item can he craft 5 times and use up all 20 leathers?

   b. Which one item can he craft 4 times and use up all 20 leathers?

   c. How many leather pieces total would Steve need to craft a full set of leather?

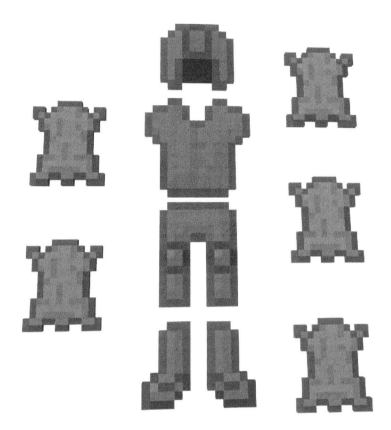

23. Now that Steve has some armor, he feels warmer and better protected. He decides to try his luck by fighting a spider. A spider has 16 hearts and Steve has 20 hearts. Spiders don't attack during the day, so Steve got the first strike. "Take this, spider!"

    a. His sword still does 5 hearts of damage. How many strikes will it take for the spider to die?

    b. The spider attacks Steve with a bite that does 2 hearts of damage. Steve got bit 4 times. How many hearts does Steve have left?

    c. The spider dropped 5 experience. If Steve wanted to gain 40 experience total, how many spiders would he need to kill?

24. "Ow! That spider's bite was painful. I should eat some food to help me recover my hearts." Steve eats some food and maxes out his hunger bar. He starts to regenerate hearts at 1 heart every 4 seconds.

   a. If he lost a total of 10 hearts from that fight, how many seconds would it take to regenerate those hearts?

   b. If Steve had only 4 hearts left after the fight and regenerated only 7 hearts, how many hearts did he end up with?

   c. What if Steve was already injured and started the fight with 15 hearts, and then the spider damaged him for 4 hearts. How many hearts is he missing from his maximum of 20?

25. The spider dropped some strings. This reminded Steve of a bow. To make a bow, Steve requires at least 3 strings and 3 sticks.

    a. If Steve has 21 strings and 15 sticks, how many bows can he make?

    b. How many strings would be left over from the question above?

    c. To make 4 sticks, Steve needs 2 wood planks. If Steve made 36 sticks, how many wood planks did he use?

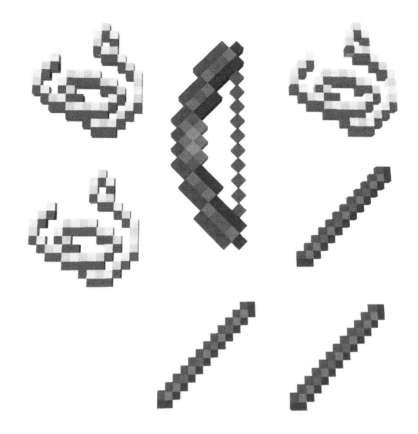

26. With a brand new bow, it is now time to make some arrows. A stack of 4 arrows would require 1 flint, 1 feather, and 1 stick.

    a. Assuming Steve has 10 flints, 5 feathers, and 4 sticks, how many arrows was he able to make?

    b. What if he had 7 flint, 7 feathers, and 7 sticks? How many arrows is that?

    c. He wants a total of 120 arrows. How many flints, feathers, and sticks would he need?

27. Armed with his new weapon, he is tempted to try it out. The sun is starting to set and Steve decides to stay outdoors to shoot some zombies. A zombie has 20 hearts and a fully charged bow can do 9 hearts of damage.

    a. How many shots would it take to kill a zombie?

    b. What about 5 zombies?

    c. What if it was an armored zombie? Steve's bow would only do 4 hearts of damage. How many shots would it take Steve to kill the armored zombie?

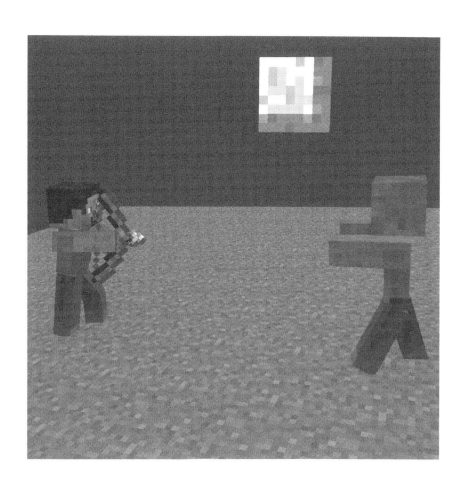

28. After killing some zombies, Steve is exhausted and goes home to sleep. He sleeps from 9 pm to 9 am.

    a. How many hours is that?

    b. If he slept only half of those hours, what time did he wake up?

    c. A zombie pounds on the door and wakes up Steve after he was sleeping for 3 hours, what time was it? He slept at 9 pm.

29. Steve wakes up restless the next morning. The zombies pounding on the door was keeping him awake at night. He decides it is time to upgrade to an iron door. He has no iron ingots, but remembers there are some in the chest at the village blacksmith building. He goes to pick up the 4 iron ingots. To make 3 iron doors, Steve would need 6 iron ingots.

   a. How many iron ingots is Steve missing to craft the iron doors?

   b. Assuming Steve has 24 iron ingots, what is the maximum amount of iron doors he can make?

   c. Assuming Steve has 30 iron ingots, but he lost 10 of them. With the remaining amount, how many doors can he craft?

   d. From the question above, how many iron ingots would be left over after crafting the doors?

30. Since Steve doesn't have enough iron ingot to craft the doors, he decides to go into town to see if a villager is willing to trade him some iron ingots. He finds the villager blacksmith who would trade 2 iron ingots for 10 leather pieces.

   a. How many leather pieces does the villager want for 1 iron ingot?

   b. Assuming the villager had 20 iron ingots to trade, how many pieces of leather would Steve need if he wanted to trade for all those ingots?

   c. Assuming Steve has 50 leather pieces and if the villager had unlimited iron ingots, how many iron ingots would Steve be able to trade?

Thank you

Congratulations! You've finished this book. Good job on solving those math problems. Stay tuned for the next volume and find out what happens to Steve. If you enjoyed this book, please leave me a review. It will help encourage me to produce these types of books in the future. Thanks!

Answers

1. a. 5 apples remaining
   b. 16 carrots left
   c. 3 gold ingots left

2. a. 15 potatoes remain
   b. 12 left
   c. 6

3. a. 10 left
   b. 8 gold ingot left
   c. 3 more apples needed

4. a. 30 seconds
   b. 150 seconds
   c. 40 blocks

5. a. 100 blocks
   b. same, 100 blocks
   c. 32 blocks

6. a. 4 windows
   b. 8
   c. 6

7. a. 80 seconds
   b. 5 blocks
   c. 60 blocks

8. a. 5 blocks of wood
   b. 7 blocks
   c. 10 blocks

9. a. 16 wood planks
    b. 28
    c. 10 max

10. a. 12 wood planks
    b. 6
    c. 24 total

11. a. 9 total
    b. 60 wood planks
    c. 12 wood planks

12. a. 3
    b. 2 more
    c. 40 total

13. a. 40
    b. 63 seconds
    c. 30 remains

14. a. 10 glasses
    b. 20
    c. 10 wood planks

15. a. 32 glass panes
    b. 11 left
    c. 6 left

16. a. 10 hours
    b. 14 hours
    c. 9 hours

17. a. 5
    b. 2 hits
    c. 20 times

18. a. 4 beds
    b. 1
    c. 15 wood planks, 15 wools

19. a. 20 raw muttons
    b. 10
    c. 7 wood planks

20. a. 2 hits
    b. 3 hides, 12 x 25% = 3
    c. 12 x 6 = 72 rabbits.

21. a. 5 leathers
    b. 28 hides
    c. 4 leathers

22. a. boots
    b. helmet
    c. 24 pieces of leather

23. a. 4 strikes
    b. 12 hearts left
    c. 8 spiders

24. a. 40 seconds
    b. 11 hearts
    c. 9

25. a. 5
    b. 6 strings left
    c. 18 wood planks

26. a. 16 arrows
    b. 28 arrows
    c. 30 flints, 30 feathers, 30 sticks

27. a. 3 shots
    b. 15 shots
    c. 5 shots

28. a. 12 hours
    b. 3 am
    c. 12 am

29. a. 2 iron ingots
    b. 12 doors
    c. 9 doors
    d. 2 left over

30. a. 5 leather pieces
    b. 100 leather pieces
    c. 10 iron ingots

Printed in Great Britain
by Amazon